Rookie

Read-About Holidays

D0204239

Independence Day

By Trudi Strain Trueit

Reading Consultant
Cecilia Minden–Cupp, PhD
Former Director of the Language and Literacy Program
Harvard Graduate School of Education
Cambridge, Massachusetts

Children's Press®
A Division of Scholastic Inc.
New York Toronto London Auckland Sydney
Mexico City New Delhi Hong Kong
Danbury, Connecticut

Designer: Herman Adler
Photo Researcher: Caroline Anderson
The photo on the cover shows a young girl participating in an Independence Day parade.

Library of Congress Cataloging-in-Publication Data

Library of Congress Cataloging-in-Publication Data
Trueit, Trudi Strain.
  Independence Day / by Trudi Strain Trueit.
    p. cm. — (Rookie read-about holidays)
  ISBN-10: 0-531-12457-6 (lib. bdg.)   0-531-11838-X (pbk.)
  ISBN-13: 978-0-531-12457-4 (lib. bdg.)   978-0-531-11838-2 (pbk.)
  1. Fourth of July—Juvenile literature. 2. Fourth of July celebrations—Juvenile literature. I. Title. II. Series.
  E286.T87 2006
  394.2634—dc22   2006003957

CHILDREN'S PRESS, and ROOKIE READ-ABOUT®, and associated logos are trademarks and/or registered trademarks of Scholastic Library Publishing. SCHOLASTIC and associated logos are trademarks and/or registered trademarks of Scholastic Inc.
1 2 3 4 5 6 7 8 9 10 R 16 15 14 13 12 11 10 09 08 07

Crack! Boom! It's Independence Day! This is when we celebrate the birthday of the United States of America.

Starting four hundred years ago, people from Europe came to live in America. They formed thirteen colonies on the east coast.

A colony is an area of land ruled by another country. These colonies were ruled by Britain, a European country.

5ᵀᴴ ROYAL IRISH DRAGOONS
DISBANDED - 1798.

1742.　　　　1751　　　　1751.

British soldiers in their red uniforms during the 1700s

Angry colonists threw tea into Boston Harbor in 1773 to protest taxes.

The British government
told the people in the
colonies to send them
money for taxes. This made
the colonists angry. They
refused to pay the taxes.

The thirteen colonies decided it was time to break free from Britain. They wanted to make their own rules. This caused the Revolutionary War to begin in America in 1775.

The British (in red coats) fighting the colonists

Thomas Jefferson

Future U.S. president
Thomas Jefferson wrote
a document called
the Declaration of
Independence. This paper
said the colonies were
no longer under British
rule. The colonies were
creating the United
States of America.

American leaders voted to accept the Declaration of Independence on July 4th, 1776. But it took seven more years before the United States was completely free from Britain's rule.

The signing of the Declaration of Independence

Fireworks still light up the sky every July 4th.

Church bells rang out in Philadelphia, Pennsylvania, on July 4th, 1777. It was the nation's first birthday. Fireworks lit up the sky. Ships fired their cannons.

These noisy Fourth of
July customs soon spread
to other cities. In 1870,
Independence Day became
a U.S. holiday.

July 2007

Sunday	Monday	Tuesday	Wednesday	Thursday	Friday	Saturday
1	2	3	4	5	6	7
8	9	10	11	12	13	14
15	16	17	18	19	20	21
22	23	24	25	26	27	28
29	30	31				

The U.S. flag is a symbol of freedom.

Ways to Celebrate

It is a custom to hang an American flag on Independence Day. The flag honors those who have died fighting for the nation's freedom.

Americans also celebrate
by getting together with
friends and family. They
gather for barbecues
and picnics.

Some families go to
parades. Others attend
concerts in parks.

Children marching together in their town's parade

The Statue of Liberty

People often take trips on the Fourth of July. They visit symbols of freedom, such as the Statue of Liberty in New York City.

Some people act out famous battles between the colonists and the British on Independence Day. Just cover your ears when the cannons roar! Boom!

A reenactment of a Revolutionary War battle

Boating on Independence Day

Boating, camping, and outdoor activities are also popular Independence Day activities. Runners in Seward, Alaska, race to the top of Mount Marathon and back.

It is traditional to end
the Fourth of July with
fireworks. Some people
watch dazzling fireworks
shows with live music.

Others are happy to
stay home. They simply
light red, white, and blue
sparklers in the backyard.

Lighting sparklers in the backyard

Words You Know

Declaration of
Independence

fireworks

flag

parades

Revolutionary War

sparklers

Statue of Liberty

Thomas Jefferson

Index

About the Author

Trudi Strain Trueit is a former television news reporter and weather forecaster. She has written more than thirty fiction and nonfiction books for children. Ms. Trueit lives near Seattle, Washington, with her husband Bill.

Photo Credits

Photographs © 2007: Corbis Images/Ariel Skelley: 3; Danita Delimont Stock Photography/Dave Bartruff: 25; Getty Images: 29 (James Cotier/Photonica), 14, 30 top right (Wayne Eastep/Stone), 9, 31 top (Hulton Archive); Masterfile: cover (Ariel Skelley), 18, 30 bottom left (Lloyd Sutton); North Wind Picture Archives: 6; Photo Researchers, NY/Richard T. Nowitz: 26; PhotoEdit: 21, 30 bottom right (Gary Conner), 22, 31 bottom left (Jonathan Nourok); Superstock, Inc.: 13, 30 top left; The Art Archive/Picture Desk: 5; The Image Works/Mary Evans Picture Library: 10, 31 bottom right.